When I Grow Up, When I Was Young
An Elementary Conversation

Bernice Seward

Copyright 2015 by Bernice Seward

All stories and artwork are copyright of their respective creators and are reproduced herein with permission.

All rights reserved. No part of this publication may be reproduced or used in any manner whatsoever without the express written permission of the publisher except for the use of brief quotations in a book review. For requests, write to Bernice Seward at PO Box 1069, Lewiston, ID 83501 or online at www.berniceseward.com.

Fonts used in this book include ERASER, Engine and Quicksand.

ISBN: 978-0-9862879-3-0

19 18 17 16 15/ 10 9 8 7 6 5 4 3 2 1

FOR OUR MOMS AND DADS – THE KINDERGARTNERS

For our parents, grandparents, family and friends – The First Graders

For Karissa and Lynn, and early elementary educators everywhere – Bernice Seward

Artists and storytellers:
Ryle, Dillan, Sophia, Silas, Jake, Logan, Aiden, Maggie, Gunner, Alex, Madyson, J.C., Jack, Rowan, Emma, TJ, Natalya, Lily, Alexandra, Kyle, Madalyn, Seth, Larry, Mattaniah, Olivia, Bianca, Carson and Sadie

Ryle

WHEN I GROW UP I WANT TO BE A RADIOLOGIST. THEY LOOK AT BONES.

I KNOW A GREAT RADIOLOGIST, AND IT'S MY DAD.

When I was young I wondered what I would be when I grew up. I thought I was going to be a doctor. Kids would be my patients.

I still want to be a doctor.

Now I wonder what I did when I was young.

I know I rode a tricycle. Now I ride a two-wheeler. It's 19 inches long. I can stand up on the pedals and jump it.

I KNOW WHAT I WANT TO BE WHEN I GROW UP.

I DON'T KNOW WHAT IT'S CALLED, BUT I KNOW WHAT THEY DO. THEY ASK CLIENTS WHAT THEY'VE DONE WRONG AND TELL THEM WHAT TO DO RIGHT.

MY DAD AND MY AUNT BETHIE DO THIS JOB. AND MY GRANDPA DOES IT.

I WANT TO BE ONE BECAUSE THEY HELP PEOPLE. IT'S GOOD TO HELP PEOPLE AND IT'S WHAT THE BIBLE SAYS TO DO.

I drew beards for us. Mine is *really* long!

When I was young I went bowling with my dad. I had to use gutter blockers and the bowling ramp for little kids.

I still go bowling with my dad. But I don't have to use the bowling ramp anymore, just the bumpers.

Also, I used to think about a giant boat with portals. I even had a dream about it.

WHEN I GROW UP I WANT TO BE A NAVY SEAL.

THEY HELP PROTECT THE COUNTRY AND CITY AND THEY TRAVEL ALL OVER THE WORLD TO KEEP IT SAFE.

Jake

NAVY SEALS CALL THEMSELVES SEALS BECAUSE THEY GO IN THE AIR, ON THE GROUND AND IN THE WATER.

I used to wonder what it was like to be in a monster truck. I played with monster truck toys when I was little because I liked them.

I don't like them as much anymore.

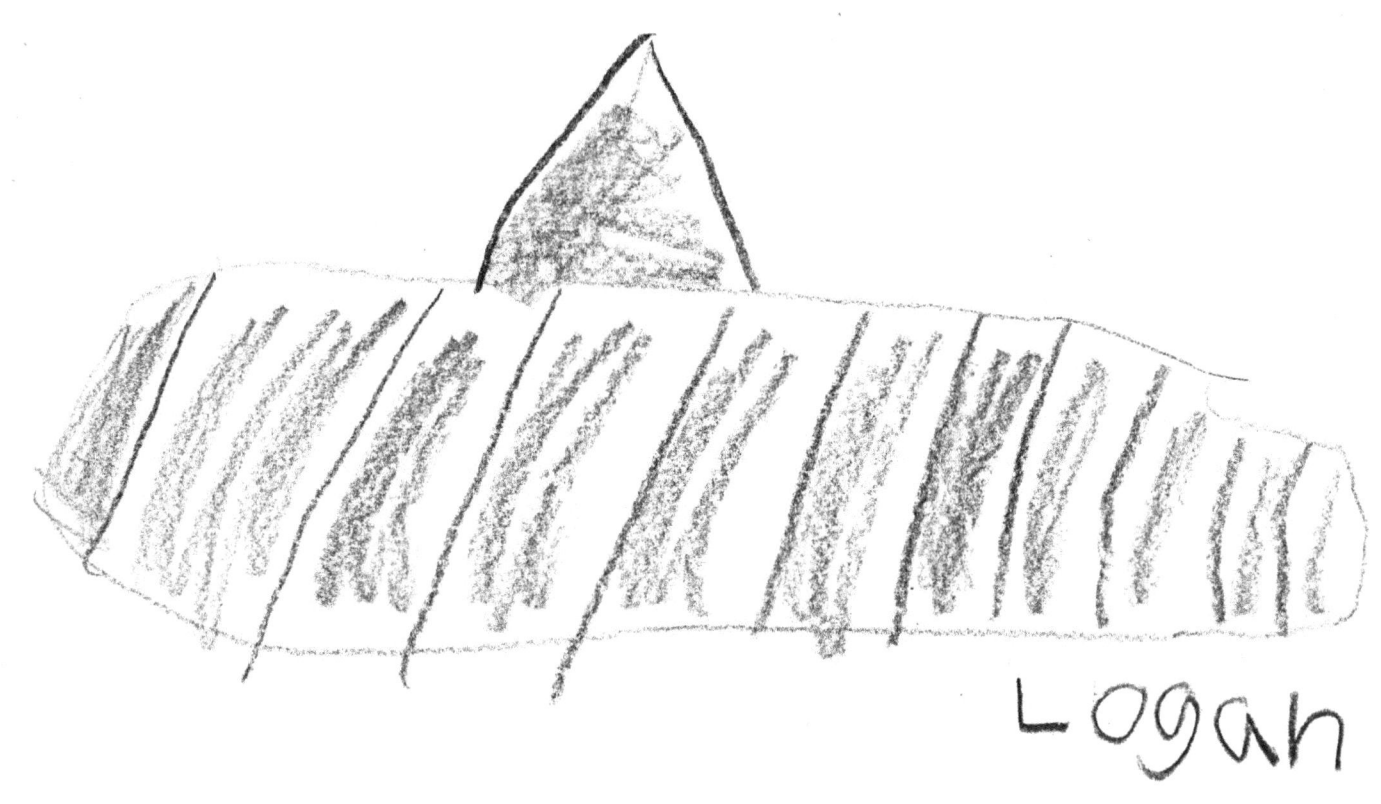

Now I wonder what it would be like to be in a submarine.

When I was young I wondered what school would be like. I thought it would be fun. Now that I'm in school, it is fun but it's kind of hard. Well, math is hard. Doing packets is easy.

When I was young I also used to cuddle with my mom. I liked that she would cuddle with me, and we still cuddle.

LOVE TOY
PEACE GENTLE
GOOD maggie niss
niss Kindniss

WHEN I GROW UP I WANT TO BE A SCIENTIST. ONE THAT HAS GLOVES AND THEY MAKE THINGS THAT ARE KIND OF LIKE WATER BUT THEY'RE PRETTY. THEY ARE COOL.

WHEN I GROW UP I ALSO WANT TO GO TO ALASKA TO SEE MY GRANDPARENTS. THEY LIVED THERE 50 YEARS.

I used to write my name like this.

Now I write my name like this.

When I was young my favorite color was yellow. Now, on top of that, I like red, orange, turquoise and aqua.

I used to need help writing my name. Sometimes I forgot how to do it. I forgot to do the lowercase "l-e-x."

I used to wonder how tall I would be when I grew up. I don't know why but I like to be tall.

Now I wonder what it would be like if I had two pairs of hands. Or 50 pairs of hands. I could do lots of things at once, like climb, color, write and hold.

WHEN I GROW UP I WANT TO GO TO DISNEYLAND BECAUSE I HAVE NOT WENT THERE YET. IT WILL BE FUN.

Madyson

WE CAN MEET OLAF AND ELSA AT DISNEYLAND. OLAF IS MY MOM'S FAVORITE, AND ELSA IS MY FAVORITE.

I remember that every day before my dad went to work he let me play with his tie. I liked to do that when I was a baby.

Now Dad lets me pull his work key. I stretch the black thing that has his picture. I pull it as far as I want and then let it go back.

WHEN I GROW UP I WANT TO BE A POLICE MAN.

THE POLICE TAKE CARE OF BAD GUYS. THEY PUT THEM IN JAIL AND GIVE TICKETS TO PEOPLE.

When I was little I used to play outside a lot. I just danced and played. Now that I'm bigger I like to play inside a lot.

IT'S KIND OF HARD TO EXPLAIN WHAT I WANT TO BE WHEN I GROW UP.

I WANT TO BE A HORSEBACK RIDER ON A FARM. I WILL HAVE COWS, CHICKENS AND SHEEP.

I used to ride my old horse, Cricket. She was a really sweet pony. I had to sell her and I didn't want to because she was so cute.

Now I ride two different horses. Their names are Cowboy and Roanie.

WHEN I GROW UP I WANT TO GO TO AFRICA. THEN I CAN TRY RIDING AN ELEPHANT LIKE MY SISTER DID. SHE WENT TO THE CIRCUS AND RODE ONE.

PLUS, I WANT TO SEE ALL THE OTHER PRETTY ANIMALS THAT ARE IN AFRICA.

When I was little I needed help crossing the street. My mom and dad helped with that, and they still do.

I loved to cuddle with my mom when I was young. We cuddled on the couch by the fire.

I used to play ring around the rosy a lot with my dolls. Their names are Rosy and Scooter. I still have my dolls. We play family. I pretend I am their mom and I cuddle with them.

I WANT TO BE A DOCTOR WHEN I GROW UP BECAUSE MY MOM SAID I WOULD BE A GOOD DOCTOR.

I LIKE TO PLAY WITH MY DOLLS. THEY ARE PATIENTS. I HAVE A LOT OF PATIENTS BECAUSE I HAVE A LOT OF DOLLS. I FIGURE OUT WHAT'S WRONG WITH THEM WHEN THEY'RE SICK. I HAVE THEM GET MEDICINE. THAT'S WHAT MY MOM DOES WHEN I'M SICK.

When I was young I played with big building blocks. Now I play with Legos. I like to build houses.

WHEN I GROW UP I WANT TO BUILD STUFF-LIKE A DOG HOUSE. AND SOMETHING FOR MY CATS.

I WILL BUILD A CAGE WITH A BIG POINTY THING ON TOP SO THE CATS HAVE A ROOF AND DON'T GET ALL WET. I'LL PUT FOOD AND WATER AND A CAT BOX IN IT. I'LL GET A PARROT, TOO. I'LL TEACH THE PARROT HOW TO TALK AND IT WILL LIVE IN THE POINTY ROOF OF THE CAT HOUSE.

When I was young I needed help getting up on high places. One time a big tank from Star Wars was on top of the entertainment center. I put my feet on big black things on the side of the entertainment center and I climbed up. I got stuck up there, and had to wait for somebody to help me down.

Seth

Also, when I was young I wondered how much it would hurt to be stung by a bee. Once there was a bee on my head but it didn't sting me. Another time I saw a bee and I jumped off my scooter and ran inside.

I like to draw Autobots. Once I made an Optimus Prime out of paper.

WHEN I GROW UP I WANT TO GO BACK IN TIME AND SAVE THE ISRAELITES FROM WORKING AS SLAVES IN EGYPT. I WOULD HAVE TO BUILD A TIME MACHINE FIRST. IT WOULD BE BIG, AND YOU WOULD HAVE TO DRILL UNDERGROUND TO GET TO IT.

When I was young I really liked to draw. I used to draw helicopters—lots of them. I also wondered what the future would be like. Like, when they were going to make hovering cars.

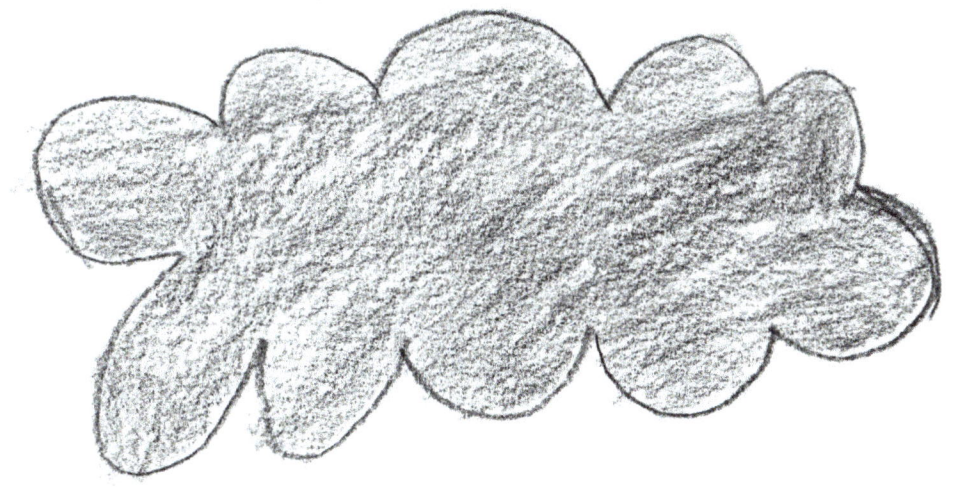

I still wonder about the hovering cars, but my dad says they're getting to that technology.

I KIND OF WANT TO BE THREE THINGS WHEN I GROW UP. NO, FOUR THINGS. WHEN I'M A MOM AND MY KIDS ARE LITTLE I WILL BE A BABYSITTER. WHEN MY KIDS ARE IN SCHOOL I WILL BE A TEACHER.

WHEN THEY ARE IN COLLEGE I WILL BE A FASHION DESIGNER. ONCE I'M DONE WITH ALL THOSE THINGS I'LL BE A BOOK WRITER.

When I was young I played outside with my sister a lot. We used to play house.

Now we play tag and hide-and-go-seek. I like to play with my sister. And plus I always win.

Bianca

I used to wonder what it would be like to be in heaven. I still don't know. But I think there might be trees in heaven. Then I can climb them. And if I jump down, I'll be okay.

Now I wonder why crackers are good for your stomach. I also wonder how you make the color white.

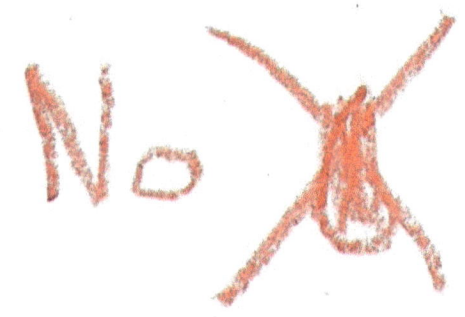

WHEN I GROW UP I DON'T WANT TO BE SOMETHING THAT HAS TO DEAL WITH BLOOD. SO I WON'T BE A DOCTOR, A FIREFIGHTER OR A POLICE OFFICER.

A PLUMBER! I'LL BE A PLUMBER WHEN I GROW UP.

THIS IS ME AS A KID. I'M DRESSED UP LIKE A PLUMBER.

I used to wonder what the world would be like when I turned seven. I thought it might be fun when I went to school, like fun to make new friends.

School is fun and I like it. I like that I have a reading buddy. I don't like homework, though. Not on Mondays, not on any days!

I used to sleep with my mommy and daddy. Now my brother Danny and I sneak into their bed. First, we peek to see where Daddy and Mommy are. Then I whisper, "Come on, Danny." And we tiptoe, open their bedroom door, open the blankets, get the blankets over us, say goodnight, and then we fall asleep!

"THE END"

Wait! There wasn't enough room to share the WHOLE conversation. Can you guess who these extra quotes are from?

1. I used to need help saddling my horse. I still need help doing that.

2. I COLOR A LOT. THAT'S WHY I'M SO GOOD AT IT.

3. I want to be a paleontologist and discover new types of dinosaurs. And I want to learn more about them.

4. One time my mom and dad wanted me to go on a roller coaster but I was scared.

5. My brother Zachary got stung one time when a bee flew up his pant leg.

6. I HAVE LEGOS AND TRANSFORMERS. I PRETEND PEOPLE ARE IN A FIRE AND THE TRANSFORMERS GRAB THEM AND BRING THEM DOWN AND SAVE THEM.

When I was little I had tons and tons of questions. When you're little you don't know that much. 7

Maybe in heaven you could jump out of trees into marshmallows. Then you could eat your way out of the marshmallows. Yum! 8

WHEN I'M A TEACHER I'LL SAY, "EVERYBODY, YOU DID SO WELL ON YOUR TEST YOU ALL GET AN A+ AND A FIELD TRIP TO A RANCH TO SEE MISS NATALYA'S HORSES." 10

When I was like five there was nothing that I wondered about. I can't remember anything. 9

I'M GONNA HAVE A CAN FOR PENCILS WHEN I GROW UP. AND A BIG PENCIL COLLECTION. 11

When I was little my mom and dad helped me feel good and they made me laugh. 12

Turn the page to see if you guessed right!

Quotes:
1. TJ
2. Alexandra
3. Mattaniah
4. Rowan
5. Seth
6. Aiden
7. Bianca
8. Maggie
9. J.C.
10. Olivia
11. Carson
12. Lily

www.ingramcontent.com/pod-product-compliance
Lightning Source LLC
Chambersburg PA
CBHW061120010526
44112CB00024B/2923